Be With You

BEYONCÉ

Publisher and Creative Director: Nick Wells
Project Editor: Polly Prior
Art Director and Layout Design: Mike Spender
Digital Design and Production: Chris Herbert

Special thanks to: Laura Bulbeck,Emma Chafer, Esme Chapman, Karen Fitzpatrick, Daniela Nava

FLAME TREE PUBLISHING
Crabtree Hall, Crabtree Lane
Fulham, London SW6 6TY
United Kingdom

www.flametreepublishing.com

First published 2013

12 14 16 15 13
1 3 5 7 9 10 8 6 4 2

A CIP record for this book is available from the British Library upon request.

ISBN 978-0-85775-991-7

Printed in China

Be With You
BEYONCÉ

CAROLINE CORCORAN

Foreword by Malcolm Mackenzie,
Editor, *We Love Pop*

**FLAME TREE
PUBLISHING**

Contents

Foreword

Beyoncé's greatest asset – aside from her voice, her moves, her songwriting abilities, her business mind and the way she fits into her Deréon jeans – is her commitment. She is focused like no other pop star, putting 100 per cent of herself into everything she does. See her incredible live shows and you'll never doubt it.

Now watch the video for 'Single Ladies (Put A Ring On It)'. Who learns impossible dance routines these days? No one. Most celebrities can't be bothered. Not Beyoncé. She sees the end game. It's

not about paying the leccy bill, or even having a quickie hit, it's about the legacy. She's in it for the long haul, but frankly Mrs Carter, you are already a legend.

Kanye West may be a buffoon, but he wasn't wrong when he stormed the 2009 MTV Awards in horror when Taylor Swift's video won over Beyoncé's groundbreaking 'Single Ladies' clip that's easily the most iconic pop video since Kylie's 'Can't Get You Out Of My Head' and '…Baby One More Time' by Britney.

Some of us mortals are slightly mistrustful of Beyoncé. Surely she's too perfect? How can a woman be this beautiful and this smart and this talented? She was amazing in Destiny's Child, she's an equally amazing solo artist, she's a flipping good actress: heck I even loved her rapping in MTV's hip-hopera *Carmen*. But B does have one weakness… a love of fabrics best suited to DFS than DKNY. But never mind that.

Who runs the world? Have you not been paying attention? She does!

Malcolm Mackenzie Editor, *We Love Pop*

R&B Sensation

Introducing Mrs Beyoncé Knowles-Carter: owner of 17 Grammys (six of them won in one night), one half of the world's only billionaire celebrity couple, 12 MTV Video Music Awards, seven *Billboard* Music Awards and four American Music Awards.

The world might not have a clue what goes on inside her home, but one thing it does know is that on her shelves there are *a lot* of awards.

Being Bey

Her success, however, goes beyond silverware: 10 singles in the UK Top 5, a 100 per cent record for her albums heading straight to the top of the US *Billboard* 200 (album chart) and, unusually for someone who is so widely successful, Beyoncé has even found critical acclaim. In 2009 iconic music brand *NME* voted 'Crazy In Love' their 'song of the decade' and defended themselves when criticized with what wasn't so much praise, as worship. And, as anyone who has ever danced to Beyoncé with a gaggle of girls at 2 am knows, that song can be a religious experience.

In the much-discussed *Forbes* lists, Beyoncé features regularly; she is No. 4 in 'The World's Most Powerful Celebrities' list, No. 17 in their '100 Most Powerful Women' list and, alongside husband Jay-Z, one half of the world's highest-paid celebrity couple.

'It makes you feel more than alive. Technically it's perfect, the ultimate tune for the holy sphere of the dancefloor.'

NME ON 'CRAZY IN LOVE'

BEYONCÉ: *Be With You*

National Treasure

When she made *Time*'s 100 Most Influential People list (this is not specific to musicians or celebrities; it includes the *entire world*), Baz Luhrmann, who worked with Beyoncé on *The Great Gatsby* soundtrack, as well as years earlier at the Academy Awards (Oscars), gave his verdict on why: 'When Beyoncé does an album, when Beyoncé sings a song, when Beyoncé does anything, it's an event, and it's broadly influential. Right now, she is the heir-apparent diva of the USA — the reigning national voice.'

It doesn't feel like an exaggeration, especially when you recall Beyoncé singing Etta James's 'At Last' at President Obama's initial swearing in or relive her performance of 'The Star Spangled Banner' at Obama's second inauguration in Washington – or remember her playing in the biggest event in US tradition: the Super Bowl. Let's not underestimate this; these are gigs that go down in history, the kind that would not go to any other current chart artist.

'The most important and compelling popular musician of the twenty-first century ... the logical end-point, of a century-plus of pop.'

JODY ROSEN, *THE NEW YORKER*

'If you work hard,
whatever you want,
it will come to you.
I know that's easier
said than done but
keep trying.'

BEYONCÉ

'The first...' is the start of many sentences about Beyoncé: the first African-American woman to win the American Society of Composers, Authors and Publishers' (ASCAP) 'Songwriter of the Year' award (in 2002) and, in 2011, the first woman to play the main stage at Glastonbury, where reports of 'the sheer visceral power of her voice' overtook any doubts that Beyoncé's brand of fierce R&B pop might not fit on a main stage normally known for its guitar bands.

Strike A Pose

Beyoncé is now more than a singer: she's a brand. She has her own clothing line, House of Deréon, as well as numerous fragrances – and it doesn't stop there, as she is also the face of household names such as H&M, L'Oréal, Pepsi, etc. It's a monster of a repertoire which shows no signs of slowing down.

Moreover, all the major photographers are constantly clamouring to shoot her for *Vogue*, *GQ* and the rest. Add to that the coverage that her interviews get – whether she talks about motherhood, love, Hurricane Katrina, feminism or what shoes she's planning to wear next week – and you'll understand why for most publications Beyoncé is a very rare breed: sexy enough for men and strong enough for women. Basically, the ultimate cover girl.

'I am really proud that I am one of the artists that has the opportunity to be on magazine covers.' BEYONCÉ

'Ever since I was an introverted kid, I'd get on stage and be able to break out of my shell.'

BEYONCÉ

Something About The Girl

Beyoncé's music knows no age limit and she is adored by all of her fans who appreciate the sort of role model she has become to young girls. Although the singer tries to keep her private life away from the spotlight, the media are always hungry for any little detail. However, you won't find embarrassing pictures of her plastered all over the front pages every day: her behaviour is impeccable.

Love To Love Her

So what is it that makes Beyoncé so ridiculously successful? Of course, part of it is natural talent – sometimes the myth of Beyoncé makes you forget that she is an amazing musician who writes her own songs and jumps across three octaves as casually as most people jump across a puddle.

The woman can invent a dance that will have everyone – from teenage girls to grown women at a hen party – united on the dancefloor. Then there is the film career, with roles in *Dreamgirls*, *Austin Powers In Goldmember* and *Cadillac Records* amongst others.

However, the Beyoncé phenomenon goes beyond talent; people just … well, they love the woman! Simon Cowell's PR machine couldn't have done such a perfect job on Beyoncé's image as she has done simply by being herself, and in a world of cynicism about celebrities – especially super-successful ones – that's saying something.

'No one has that voice, no one moves the way she moves, no one can hold an audience the way she does.'

BAZ LUHRMANN

> *'I don't like to gamble but if there's one thing I am willing to bet on it's myself.'*
>
> BEYONCÉ

Brand Beyoncé

So how does she do it? Partly, it's the clean living image – we do not see Beyoncé falling out of clubs, heading to rehab or swearing on Twitter. We have never seen a Beyoncé mugshot or read scandals about her marriage.

Instead, we see a grown-up who appreciates what she has and works hard – the evidence is in the new album, the high-octane tour – and we know that, despite the glamorous lifestyle, Bey (she would almost definitely want us to call her Bey) puts the hours in … which brings us on to that new moniker.

Part of Bey's popularity *has* to lie in her marriage to Jay-Z: the man for whom she took the name Carter (she now officially goes by Knowles-Carter). That's not taking anything away from Beyoncé herself, but when choosing a partner – deliberately or not – she sent out a message. She made it clear that she wanted a husband who was her equal, and her fans respected her all the more for that. After their marriage in 2008, Beyoncé and Jay-Z became the ultimate music power couple.

Baby Bey

In January 2012, Beyoncé gave birth to a daughter, Blue Ivy, after a suitably dramatic pregnancy reveal: just as she went to pose for photographers at the 2011 MTV Video Music Awards (VMAs) on the red carpet, Beyoncé smiled sweetly, cradled her stomach and said she had a secret.

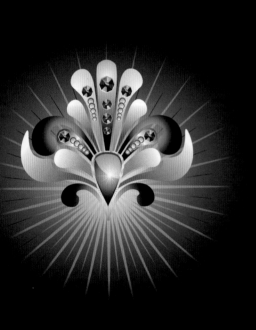

MTV then tweeted, saying, 'OMG Beyoncé just made a huge announcement on the #vma carpet! #baby!!!!' before Bey's rep confirmed the news, declaring: 'I'm happy to say it's true.' The news broke Twitter records, with 8,868 tweets per second following the announcement.

Inside, Beyoncé threw her microphone on the floor and ripped open her blazer after a performance of 'Love On Top', saying 'I want you to feel the love that's growing inside me.'

As she sings in 'Run The World (Girls)', Beyoncé was definitely 'strong enough to bear the children then get back to business'.

At the same time, it seemed as though Beyoncé began to transcend the music industry. Wife, mother, actress and, suddenly, she had a new persona which was, in her own words to British *Vogue*, 'modern-day feminist'.

She sparked some controversy when she told *GQ* in early 2013 that 'equality is a myth'. The feminist points, though, featured inside; on the cover, Beyoncé was exposing her breasts.

Who Does She Love?

As is the case for all artists, Beyoncé has been influenced by other singers – some older ones who have recently passed away and others, more recent ones, who only encountered success not too long ago. However, despite her young age, Bey is finding that, increasingly, *she* has become the role model for girls to look up to for inspiration.

Bingeing On Beats

Beyoncé has admitted that as a child she was introverted; well, being in a pop group managed by her dad from aged eight meant that there wasn't much time for teenage partying.

So while other teenagers binged on beer, Beyoncé binged on music: Diana Ross, Whitney, Aretha … You don't become an artist like Beyoncé without having a genuine passion for music and other musicians, and she spent her youth soaking up the influence of the greats. Indeed, Beyoncé is the first to pay homage to these amazing singers and to credit them with the influence they had on her.

She believes that Michael Jackson helped her to become the artist she is today, and when Whitney Houston and Donna Summer both passed away in 2012, Beyoncé paid a musical tribute to them both on stage in Atlantic City.

'Diana Ross is a big inspiration to all of us. We all grew up watching everything about her … her class.'

BEYONCÉ ON DIANA ROSS

'She's been a huge and constant part of my life as an artist since I was about 10 or 11.'

ADELE ON BEYONCÉ

Listening To Houston In Houston

Beyoncé had earlier spoken not only of Whitney's musical genius but also of her personal kindness and sincerity; she grew up singing Whitney songs and felt that the doors had been opened for her by Whitney's career. And there were older influences than Whitney. 'Playing Etta James taught me so much about myself, and singing her music inspired me to be a stronger artist,' Beyoncé wrote on her official website after the death of the legendary artist. Then there are the more modern influences; it's hard not to listen to early Destiny's Child and hear a hint of TLC and En Vogue.

'She was the ultimate legend ... Her voice was perfect. Strong but soothing. Soulful and classic. Her vibrato, her cadence, her control.'

BEYONCÉ ON WHITNEY HOUSTON

For Beyoncé, the influences on her music are constantly changing and evolving. 'I started off being inspired by [Afrobeat music pioneer] Fela Kuti ... I also found a lot of inspiration in '90s R&B, Earth, Wind & Fire, DeBarge, Lionel Richie, Teena Marie,' she said about making the album *4* (2011). 'I listened to a lot of Jackson 5 and New Edition, but also Adele, Florence + the Machine and Prince. Add in my hip-hop influences, and you can hear how broad it is.'

> *You could hear his soul … It was so raw and so pure … It's something that's God given … Michael Jackson changed me.'*
>
> BEYONCÉ ON MICHAEL JACKSON

Girl Crush

The irony is, of course, that many of Beyoncé's more modern influences are artists who have also been influenced *by* her.

Adele has been outspoken about her girl crush on Bey, telling *Vogue* in 2013: 'I love how all of her songs are about empowerment. Even when she's married and Jay-Z put a ring on it, she releases "Single Ladies". Go get yours. Go get what you deserve. I think she's really inspiring.'

The one that's interesting, perhaps, is Rihanna. Jay-Z's protégée and natural predecessor to Beyoncé's crown, she doesn't keep quiet about many things, but her relationship with Beyoncé is one of them.

She did tweet a response to a picture of Beyoncé, taken not long after she'd become a mother to Blue Ivy, saying: 'This pic could single-handedly destroy the self-esteem of an entire nation.' For someone as cool as Rihanna, that is one hell of a compliment. And she's not the only one in awe of the woman who does, seemingly, get it right all the time.

During the Super Bowl 2013 show, some huge pop names took to Twitter to praise Beyoncé's performance. Alicia Keys sung her praises and P Diddy deemed her his 'f**kin hero'. Jessie J said that Bey was a superstar 'to her fingertips'. Perhaps the last word, though, should go to Justin Timberlake, who sums it up in that oh-so-succinct twenty-first century style: '#QUEENBEY'.

'I'm with my mother who reminds me, "Girl, you are not a Queen." So it's good to have some balance.'

BEYONCÉ

Beyoncé Giselle Knowles

Beyoncé's family have been involved from the very beginning in her career and have always been really supportive. As is often the case, though, relationships can go wrong, and Bey has had to overcome the trauma of her parents' very public divorce. However, the women in her family remain incredibly close and the next generation's chance of future success looks very promising!

Beyincé To Beyoncé

Beyoncé started life as a usual Texas girl, with an unusual Texas name. *Beyoncé* is actually a homage to her mum Tina's maiden name, Beyincé, which may provide a clue to Bey's early feminist influences. Tina didn't just refuse to let go of that name, which was about to die out; she kept hold of it and then sent it stratospheric.

However, before that happened, Beyoncé Knowles lived an anonymous and happy life. In fact, Bey is quick to correct anyone who suggests she had it tough upbringing. 'I grew up in a very nice house in Houston, went to private school all my life and I've never even been to the "hood",' she once said. 'Not that there's anything wrong with the "hood".'

> *My life was work. I didn't really even go to a prom. Well, I went to my boyfriend's prom. But I had to be home early!'*

BEYONCÉ ON HER TEENAGE YEARS

Singing and dancing from an early age, it was actually her dance teacher that spotted Beyoncé's potential. As a seven-year-old, she was then entered into a talent contest, where she won for her performance of John Lennon's 'Imagine', despite competing against children who were over twice her age. Second place? You get the impression it was never an option for Beyoncé.

After that Bey's life took a different turn, as she focused on music at the Parker Elementary School in Houston (singing solos with the school choir) and then the High School for the Performing and Visual Arts.

Knowles The Rules

Beyoncé had dreams of being a singer-songwriter, and her parents supported her all the way – even by becoming part of her workforce. While Beyoncé's mum Tina – previously a costume designer and hair stylist – became her stylist, her dad Mathew, who already worked in the music business, became her manager.

In 2009, however, the Knowles family was rocked, as Mathew and Tina split up and it emerged that Mathew had fathered a child (a little boy named Nixon) with actress AlexSandra Wright. At first he denied the claims, but a paternity test proved that he was definitely the child's dad.

Mathew and Beyoncé's professional relationship also ended in 2011 with Beyoncé telling *Oprah* in 2013 that they simply had

> '*If you want to see the Third Ward Texas come out in me, disrespect my sister, and I will go completely crazy on you.*'
>
> BEYONCÉ

'issues' over who was in control. Beyoncé has reportedly never met her half-brother, despite him being close in age to her little girl, Blue Ivy.

She opened up further about it in her 2013 documentary 'Life Is But A Dream', explaining that juggling a professional and personal life became difficult and that she needed Mathew as a father. Sadly, she admitted that things had worked differently and that she 'had to let it go'.

Sister, Sister

Bey's relationships with the men in her family may be complicated, but her closeness to the women – her mum, her cousin Kelly Rowland and her sister Solange – remains constant. In fact, the siblings' relationship is so tight that one of the internet's craziest Beyoncé rumours is that the singer is actually Solange's mum, despite Beyoncé being only five years older than her little sister!

Back in the real world, when Solange – a successful singer-songwriter in her own right – split up with Daniel Smith (the father of her child who she married aged 17) there was only one woman she turned to: her big sister.

Now Solange's son, Daniel Julez, and Bey's little girl are 'more like sister and brother than cousins' – and who knows what awaits the next generation of Knowles children? Anyone for Destiny's Grandchild?

Girls Aloud

The road to forming the group Destiny's Child was not an easy one and proved just how determined Beyoncé was to achieve success. Of course, the lawsuits, accusations and divisions in the original line-up took their toll on Bey but, thankfully, the end of such a difficult journey was fast approaching.

Not Their Tyme

If Destiny's Child is synonymous with Beyoncé, consider this: they almost never existed – by that name at least.

Originally, Beyoncé and the girls went by the name Girl's Tyme, made up of Bey, her cousin Kelly Rowland and LaTavia Roberson, who Beyoncé had met at an audition, plus a few others who wouldn't be around for long. The girls were soon booked for a spot on talent show *Star Search*.

'We were kind of nervous about it,' LaTavia said afterwards. 'They made us do a rap song, although we wanted to sing.' They lost but, hey, so did Justin Timberlake and Britney Spears, so they were not in bad company.

In 1993, during years of line-up changes, LeToya Luckett joined the band and the girls were signed by Elektra Records but dropped before they got to release any material.

'Anybody that met us could see that me and Kelly were one group and they were another. It was obvious.'

BEYONCÉ

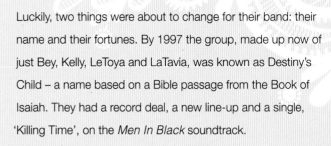

'*You could tell it was a really good chemistry. We were like sisters immediately ... it was like magic.*'

LETOYA LUCKETT ON DESTINY'S CHILD

Luckily, two things were about to change for their band: their name and their fortunes. By 1997 the group, made up now of just Bey, Kelly, LeToya and LaTavia, was known as Destiny's Child – a name based on a Bible passage from the Book of Isaiah. They had a record deal, a new line-up and a single, 'Killing Time', on the *Men In Black* soundtrack.

Dancefloor Domination

The next few years saw the group's success increase, as they claimed their first No. 1 single: the anthem of many 1990s R&B dancefloors 'Bills, Bills, Bills'.

However, by the time the next single 'Say My Name' was released, original members LaTavia and LeToya were no longer in the band – something that, according to LaTavia, they only found out when they saw the video for the single, which featured two girls named Farrah and Michelle in their places.

So what had led to such a messy situation? Well, prior to the video being released, LaTavia and LeToya had tried to fire Mathew Knowles via letter, believing that he was the cause of favouritism in the band and disliking his management style. They'd been clear that they didn't want to leave Destiny's Child but believed something needed to change with their management. The consequence? Mathew continued to manage Destiny's Child, while LaTavia and LeToya were thrown out, causing them to take out a lawsuit against their former manager. And it was at this point that things started to turn nasty.

Dark Days

While LaTavia gave interviews about Mathew Knowles being the cause of the split, Beyoncé of course saw it differently, telling *Vibe* magazine that the girls had 'lost focus'.

'They didn't want to do interviews, rehearse, or take voice lessons,' she said, adding more harshly that LeToya was 'tone deaf'. In the press, it was Beyoncé – the manager's daughter, lead singer and golden child – who was painted as the villain and the abuse took its toll; she admitted later that the fallout, which coincided with a relationship break-up, led to a depression.

'I didn't eat,' she told *Parade* magazine. 'I stayed in my room. I was in a really bad place in life, going through that lonely period: "Who am I? Who are my friends?" My life changed.'

In the end, the case between Beyoncé's dad and LaTavia and LeToya was settled out of court. The girls were gone; unfortunately for them, though, at a time when Destiny's Child were on the precipice of becoming one of the biggest girl groups of all time.

'I only allow myself one day to feel sorry for myself. People who complain really get on my nerves.'

BEYONCÉ

'I am convinced that if it was not for Mathew Knowles we would still be together as a band.'

LATAVIA ROBERSON

Supremely Talented

With a successful album under their belt, you'd think that the girls could finally relax and enjoy their new-found success. Alas, this didn't turn out to be quite the case; the loss of a further band member and the remaining girls beginning to drift in different directions signalled the end of Destiny's Child – still, who knows what the future held?

Girl Band Survivors

'That was our turning point and we all knew it,' said Beyoncé about the group signing for Columbia Records in 1997. And, as with a lot of things, Beyoncé was right.

After the initial line-up wobbles, the group found their feet, got that crucial backing from Columbia and sprinted off into the girl band history books.

After 'Say My Name', the hits kept coming, with 'Jumpin, Jumpin' – the final single from *The Writing's on the Wall* (1999) – and then the next album, *Survivor* (2001), which made No. 1s from every single released from it: 'Bootylicious', 'Survivor', 'Emotion' and 'Independent Women Part I'. The latter also saw Destiny's Child featuring on the movie soundtrack to *Charlie's Angels*. The album was critically received too, with music writers talking of a 'rare individuality, and a hint of genius'.

Taking The Lead

And was it simply a coincidence that the more successful the girls got, the bigger the role of one woman: Miss Beyoncé Knowles? Of course not!

By the time the girls made *Survivor*, Beyoncé – as well as being firmly in place as the lead singer – was instrumental behind the scenes too, writing, producing and composing what would go on to be a Grammy award-winning album.

Unfortunately, as was the way with Destiny's Child, while the music side of things was booming, personal relationships were struggling. New member Farrah Franklin – who had met the girls when performing as an extra on the 'Bills, Bills, Bills' video – would only last six months, with Beyoncé blaming missed gigs and 'disinterest' for her dismissal.

'I just hope people don't get sick of us. I'm sick of us and I'm in Destiny's Child.' BEYONCÉ

However, Michelle Williams became the final piece in the Destiny's Child puzzle and formed part of the line-up that would see the trio go down in history as one of the biggest girl bands of all time. When the group reunited for 2013's Super Bowl performance and a comeback album, the *Love Songs* (2013), Michelle (recommended to Beyoncé and Kelly

'No matter what happens, we will always love each other as friends and sisters and will always support each other.'

DESTINY'S CHILD AFTER THEIR SPLIT

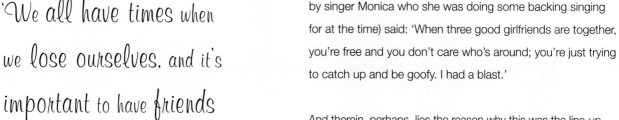

'We all have times when we lose ourselves, and it's important to have friends around who are honest with us.'

BEYONCÉ

by singer Monica who she was doing some backing singing for at the time) said: 'When three good girlfriends are together, you're free and you don't care who's around; you're just trying to catch up and be goofy. I had a blast.'

And therein, perhaps, lies the reason why this was the line-up that stuck. Kelly, Beyoncé and Michelle? They were actual friends.

The Beginning Of The End

Before the comeback, though, there must inevitably be the split, which happened in 2005, following the release of *Destiny Fulfilled* (2004) – perhaps the group's most eagerly awaited album.

Who doesn't remember hearing 'Lose My Breath' for the first time after the group's hiatus – the girls had been working on solo material and Beyoncé had even had the monster hit 'Crazy In Love' in the interim – and breathing a sigh of relief. They still had it: Destiny's Child lived on.

However, although fans were mostly satisfied, critics were divided and the album seemed to mark a natural beginning of the end for the group. A Christmas album and a tour followed, and then Destiny's Child went their separate ways.

'After a lot of discussion and some deep soul searching, we realized that our current tour has given us the opportunity to leave Destiny's Child on a high note,' the girls told a devastated crowd in Barcelona. And with that, Destiny's Child were done … but only, of course, for the moment.

Me, Myself And I

Beyoncé's first steps as a solo artist were anything but tentative: she encountered immediate success and dispelled any doubt over her ability to thrive on her own. This also became a time of personal growth when a rather naïve Beyoncé not only continued to sing about love – she actually began to experience it.

'They told me I didn't have one hit on my album. I guess they were kind of right. I had five!'

BEYONCÉ ON DANGEROUSLY IN LOVE

Going Solo

'Sasha Fierce (Bey's alter ego) was born when I did "Crazy In Love",' Beyoncé told *People* magazine in 2008 – and that's kind of obvious. Yes, Beyoncé was cool in Destiny's Child but when she went solo, something happened to propel her into another league. What Beyoncé was proving with 'Crazy In Love' was that she also had the stage presence to be a solo artist.

It wasn't like she hadn't had tasters of solo success. In 2002 Beyoncé made her first moves away from the girls as she got involved with the film *Austin Powers In Goldmember*, recording the track 'Work It Out' for the soundtrack and starring in the film as Foxxy Cleopatra. In 2003 she had also worked on the track 'Bonnie and Clyde' with Jay-Z: the man who was to become her husband and the father of her child.

However, 'Crazy In Love' was somehow different and seemed to mark the real beginning of Beyoncé: the solo artist. Everything about the single was iconic, especially the fact that

it was a collaboration between Beyoncé and Jay-Z – at the time rumoured to be her boyfriend and therefore adding some intrigue to that sexually charged performance.

Staying Solo

'Crazy In Love' won two Grammys, went to No. 1 in multiple countries and was critically lauded. When the album *Dangerously In Love* (2003) was released, the hits kept coming. First of all, the dancehall-influenced 'Baby Boy' which featured Sean Paul flew to No. 1 in the *Billboard* Hot 100 and stayed there for an epic nine weeks.

Then came the single 'Me, Myself and I', followed by 'Naughty Girl' – both not quite the monster hits of the first two but solid releases nonetheless; Beyoncé had just set the bar extremely high. *Dangerously In Love* went to No. 1 in the US, the UK and around the world, going multi-platinum and earning Beyoncé five Grammys. If there had been any doubts, this album answered them: Beyoncé was more than up to the job of being a solo artist.

Finding Her Feet

For Beyoncé this time in her life was also about finding herself. She admits that she had led a sheltered life: she'd had the same boyfriend from the age of 13 to 17 and they didn't live together or 'you know ...' And that after that, the only man

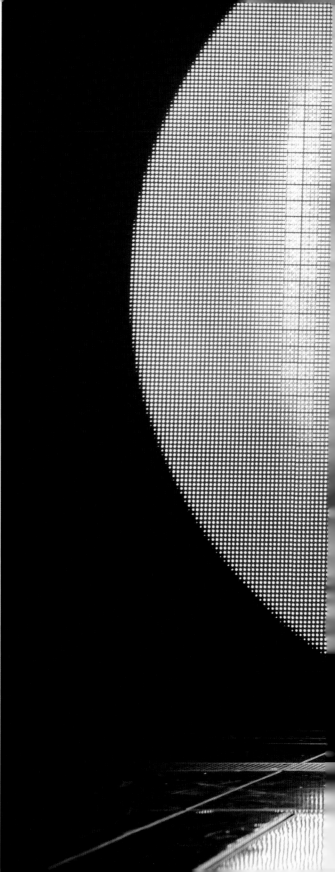

'*I feel like I'm highly respected, which is more important than any award or any amount of records.*'

BEYONCÉ

in her life was Jay-Z, whom she started dating at around the age of 19.

As for her songs, where does all that life experience come from? Well, Beyoncé dug into the recesses of her mind and pulled out memories she remembered from the days she had spent in her mum's salon when growing up: tales that the ladies in there told as they had their hair permed, trimmed or curled.

'I wrote my lyrics from growing up in my mother's hair salon and hearing stories from women there,' she told the *Telegraph*. 'Women would come in and they'd talk about what was going on in their lives. I would hear about this woman who was shy, and this woman who liked men with money, and this one's into football players, and this woman's been married 20 years and her husband's doing this and that … Those were the stories I heard.'

However, after all those years of listening to other people's life experiences, it was time for Beyoncé to start having her own.

'*I'm over being a pop star. I don't want to be a hot girl. I want to be iconic.*'

BEYONCÉ

'Love is something that never goes out of style. It's something everybody experiences ... people usually want to feel that.'

BEYONCÉ

Soul Survivor

Although they had to endure a bit of a wait, Beyoncé's fans were not left disappointed by her second album. Moreover, they soon discovered that they would have the chance to see her in person, as she began the tour that would take her all around the world. And that wasn't all: the singer proved that her talents weren't restricted simply to the world of music, as she also demonstrated that she was an excellent actress.

Yo Shorty, It's Her B'Day

It was her twenty-fifth birthday and Destiny's Child were now officially part of Beyoncé's past – not her present. Therefore, with the release of the commonly deemed 'difficult second album' – the sweetly titled *B'Day* (2006) – the singer wasn't just dipping a toe into solo stardom but rather diving headfirst.

It had been a long time coming. Originally intended to come out shortly after *Dangerously In Love*, *B'Day* was delayed by Beyoncé's focus on Destiny's Child and on her film career, as she had just finished making *Dreamgirls*: the story of an all-female group in the 1960s. Beyoncé played Deena Jones, the lead singer married to the manager of the group who emotionally abuses her.

> '*I wanted to sell a million records, and I sold a million records. I wanted to go platinum; I went platinum.*'
>
> BEYONCÉ

The film, which saw Beyoncé nominated in the Best Actress category at the Golden Globes, also produced the single 'Listen'. The track was Oscar-nominated, though Beyoncé herself missed out on a nomination, owing to a technicality over the number of names on the writing credits.

B'Day – made straight after Beyoncé finished filming – was very influenced by *Dreamgrirls*, as the singer explained: 'Because I was so inspired by Deena, I wrote songs that were saying all the things I wish she would have said in the film.'

Deja Vu?

B'Day was finished quickly and although it gave Bey six hit singles, including 'Deja Vu', 'Irreplaceable' and 'Beautiful Liar', it was the subject of mixed reviews.

While some publications praised the vocals and the epic tracks, others were left disappointed. Music journalist Peter Robinson wrote for the *Guardian* that the album 'could have been released at any point in the last three-and-a-half years … it already sounds stale'.

Despite the negative critique, *B'Day* flew off the shelves and the album launched straight to the top of the *Billboard* 200, mirroring its predecessor *Dangerously In Love*. It was also nominated for six Grammys, with Bey walking – actually, probably strutting – away with the award for 'Best Contemporary R&B Album'.

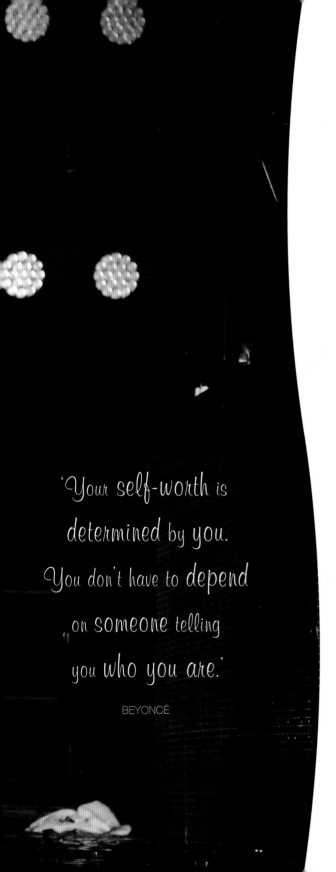

'Your self-worth is determined by you. You don't have to depend on someone telling you who you are.'

BEYONCÉ

Sasha Fierce

An exciting year was awaiting Beyoncé in 2008, when she managed to show both her tough and softer sides. The former was obvious in what she produced during her collaboration with Lady Gaga, whereas the latter clearly shone through when wedding bells rang for her and Jay-Z in an intimate New York ceremony.

The Bride Wore ... Well, Who Knows?

In a marquee on the terrace of Jay-Z's New York penthouse on Friday, 4 April 2008, Beyoncé, dressed in a sweetheart-neckline dress with a huge train made by her mum, became Mrs Knowles-Carter. The couple had dated for seven years before tying the knot; Beyoncé had always sworn she wouldn't marry before 25 – and, indeed, she was 26 on her wedding day.

Beyoncé and her family were so intent on privacy that they reportedly even shunned outside caterers, serving home-cooked food to their guests instead. There would be no magazine deals or interviews, either; in fact, it would be three years before the world would even get to see the dress, in a montage of personal photos in Beyoncé's 'I Was Here' video. Compare that to normal celebrities – with Twitter and Instagram the wait is barely three minutes.

And the dress was not the start of a big reveal; as ever with Beyoncé and Jay-Z, the rest remained private. Instead of focusing on magazine deals and gushing interviews about her big day, Beyoncé simply got on with the business of being a musician. This time taking inspiration from that on-stage alter ego 'Sasha Fierce' again, she was back with album number three, entitled *I am ... Sasha Fierce* (2008).

The album expanded on this idea of Beyoncé's bad girl alter ego: the sexy hard-edged stage performer who bore little resemblance to the good Christian girl from Houston. It was a strong concept and it had a swagger about it that seemed to reflect the confidence that Beyoncé was feeling at that moment.

Putting A Ring On It

From the album came 'If I Were a Boy', 'Halo' and, perhaps most importantly, 'Single Ladies (Put A Ring On It)'. The latter did not just become the anthem of girls' nights out across the world but also spurned arguably the most well-known dance craze of the century – before Psy came along with 'Gangnam Style', of course.

And it was no coincidence that this call to arms came following Beyoncé's own marriage. She might not be speaking ostensibly about her life change but she was acknowledging it in the way she felt comfortable with: through her music. There was no easing up following her wedding either; later that year, her world tour was announced and in the spring of 2009 she was on the road.

'I only have to follow my heart and concentrate on what I want to say to the world. I run my world.'

BEYONCÉ'S FACEBOOK

'I created my stage persona to protect myself so that when I go home I don't have to think about what it is I do.'

BEYONCÉ

All The Pop Ladies

Next up? A collaboration with perhaps the biggest star on the planet at that moment – one Miss Lady Gaga – of course. And, wow, was that collaboration iconic! 'Telephone' was a perfect pop track – feisty, catchy and critically lauded – and it went to No. 1 in numerous countries, including the UK.

A nine-minute video was more like a short film, with a strong story arc, clear artistic influences and powerful characters. The film was criticized for its levels of violence – it shows Beyoncé breaking Gaga out of prison before they kill the guests having breakfast at a diner – but praised by fans. Beyoncé seemed to be developing something of a risk-taking edge.

Gaga would later return the favour – if guest starring on one of her videos can be called such a thing – by appearing on Beyoncé's 'Video Phone'. Again, that newfound edge was evident as Beyoncé writhed around on the floor and grabbed her own breasts while eyeballing the camera. Mrs Knowles-Carter? She was pretty sexy.

'I was … 19 when we started dating. There was no rush. No one expected me to run off and get married.'

BEYONCÉ

Silver Screen

A woman of many talents, Beyoncé's attempt at breaking into the world of cinema has so far returned mixed results. Knowing how determined she is, though, it's fair to say that it won't be long before she reaches the success that she deserves … and her very good friend Gwyneth Paltrow should be able to provide plenty of useful advice.

The New Girl

They call them triple-threats – celebrities who can sing, dance and act – and Beyoncé has marked herself out as the epitome of them. No one who has seen those amazing facial expressions when she takes to the stage on tour can be surprised that she showed such an aptitude for acting. If the Mrs Carter tour showed us anything, it was that Beyoncé's face is *extremely* expressive.

Perhaps what *has* been a surprise, though, is that Beyoncé – a woman used to being at the very top – has not quite made it in the movies in the way she probably would have liked. First up came her role in *Carmen: A Hip Hopera* in 2001 where, ironically, she played an aspiring actress, but the film got average reviews. The role was followed by light-hearted parts alongside Mike Myers in *Austin Power In Goldmember* and Cuba Gooding Jr. in *The Fighting Temptations* (2003). Beyoncé was doing fine in the acting world, but that elusive breakthrough hadn't happened yet.

'I wanted to do something darker but when I got the script I thought, wow – this is heavy. Can I do this?'

The Big Break?

Perhaps *Dreamgirls* – the story of a female pop group in the 1960s and of a controlling, abusive manager – was the one that was most expected to give Beyoncé kudos in the acting world. And maybe it would have, if she had not been overshadowed, according to most reviewers, by a young girl starting out, by the name of Jennifer Hudson. The film was the making of Jennifer, who won a Best Supporting Actress Oscar for it. Meanwhile, Beyoncé received mixed reviews, despite obtaining a Golden Globe nomination.

In 2008's *Cadillac Records*, Beyoncé, who played Etta James, hinted at more depth to come from her acting but, again, the praise was not forthcoming. One reviewer said that Beyoncé was 'yet to prove any real charisma onscreen'.

Friends In High Places

Despite the shaky start in her acting career, it seems inevitable that Beyoncé will make it in Hollywood, partly thanks to her sheer determination – who can imagine her failing at anything she put her mind to? And also partly because she has the right inroads: she is a regular on Oscar red carpets and friends with the A-list. Gwyneth Paltrow is one of Beyoncé's closest confidantes and once even described how they have their best nights 'when we are just sitting around in sweatpants, having a glass of wine, chatting about life'.

Moreover, as ever with Beyoncé, there is an impressive tenacity there. Despite being busy – beyond busy, by anyone's standards – Beyoncé keeps plugging away within the movie world, including working on the soundtrack to *The Great Gatsby* with a re-recording of Amy Winehouse's 'Back to Black'.

In 2013, Beyoncé also saw the release of 3-D animated movie *Epic*, where she provided the voice of Queen Tara, the ruler of the forest where teenager M. K. (Amanda Seyfried) is suddenly transported. It's a bit of a departure but one that makes sense when Beyoncé places it in the context of the arrival of children into her life.

'I thought, "You know, by the time this comes out my daughter will … understand it's my voice and what an incredible, cool point,"' she said. 'It has so much depth. You know, it's so emotional. And I literally, I was crying when I — when I did the voiceover. And it was the first thing I did after giving birth.'

It's clearly something different for Beyoncé, but when has she ever been afraid of something new?

'I put six months aside, I've never spent six months … on doing anything … so that was a big sacrifice.'

BEYONCÉ ON DREAMGIRLS

'Sometimes it's overwhelming. Why did God give me my talent, my gift, my family. But I know you're not supposed to question God.'

BEYONCÉ IN 'I AM WORLD

TOUR' DOCUMENTARY

'Beyoncé is the most talented human being on the planet. She has so much mastery over what she does.'

GWYNETH PALTROW ON BEYONCÉ

Labour Of Love

It was a more relaxed and mature Bey who released the album *4* and also embraced motherhood. Moreover, even though she still guarded her private life very closely, she decided to share with the public certain details of some incredibly painful times in her life: a past miscarriage and the professional split from her dad, who had been her manager since the very beginning of her musical career.

4ever

In 2010, the Beyoncé juggernaut did something we had never seen it do before: it took a break. Beyoncé went to all the countries she had visited but not really seen, had a normal 9–5 routine and even tried to learn to cook, although she confessed that that did not come naturally to her – except for oxtail, which she proved oddly skilled at. 'It was great to be a wife and travel,' she said.

As is her way, though, in the hiatus Beyoncé still achieved and worked – she started a production company and directed a DVD. And when she returned to her day job, working on her new album *4*, she was refreshed and clearly inspired.

The album title also had a special place in Bey's heart, as the number 4 is her, Jay's and her mum's birth date, as well as her wedding day. She and Jay also have matching tattoos of the digit in roman numerals on their ring fingers.

'Her birth was emotional and extremely peaceful, we are in heaven ... We are thankful to everyone for all your prayers.'

BEYONCÉ ON BLUE IVY'S BIRTH

On its release, *4* headed straight to the top of the *Billboard 200*. The first single from it, 'Run the World (Girls)' was another standout female anthem. Followed by 'Best Thing I Never Had', 'Countdown' and that warbly classic 'Love on Top', *4* was delivering the hits.

The Break-up

Interestingly, this was the point when Beyoncé finally severed professional ties with her father after 20 years. She addressed the split in her 2013 documentary 'Life Is But A Dream', saying: 'I feel like I had to move on, and not work with my dad. And I don't care if I don't sell one record. It's bigger than the record, it's bigger than my career.'

It marked a new perspective for Beyoncé; she had achieved more than most artists do in a lifetime and now she could do what *she* wanted. And the next thing she chose to do was a series of intimate gigs – four of them, of course – in New York. The gigs sold out in 22 seconds and were critically praised, especially considering that these were far different circumstances from what Beyoncé was used to: performing for crowds of only a few thousand was like playing for a few mates round at her place over a bottle of Sauv Blanc.

The Real Bey?

Beyoncé was doing it her way, enjoying life, and never more so than when, in January 2012, her little girl arrived. This was a brave new world for Beyoncé, who decided to give her fans a glimpse of it by making 'Life Is But A Dream'.

'I needed boundaries, and I think my dad needed boundaries … I needed a break. I needed my dad.'

BEYONCÉ ON ENDING WORKING

RELATIONSHIP WITH HER DAD

Was Beyoncé chilling out? The documentary – a very revealing thing to do for someone so private – showed her barefoot, relaxing at home with her family ... albeit pretty stage-managed, since she did of course produce and direct it.

She opened up, though, and also on extremely confessional subjects, including her feelings for her husband, as she told him: 'Every year, I'm even more in love with you.' But by far the most personal moment of the documentary came when Beyoncé – following Jay-Z's revelation in the track 'Glory' that they had lost a baby prior to having Blue – discussed her miscarriage.

'Literally the week before I went to the doctor, everything was fine, but there was no heartbeat,' she said in the documentary. 'I went into the studio and wrote the saddest song I've ever written in my life ... It was the best form of therapy for me, because it was the saddest thing I've ever been through.'

'If you don't take the time to think about and analyse your life you'll never realize all the dots that are all connected.'

BEYONCÉ

'I did it for my sanity, my life, my relationships, my nephew, my husband, my sister and my friendships.'

BEYONCÉ ON TAKING TIME OUT

Mrs Carter vs Beyoncé

It can't be easy to find the right balance between the desire to have a private life away from the spotlight and being a public figure adored by millions of people who crave any titbit of gossip. Beyoncé, however, seems to have done just that: her family life is shielded from the media glare and her fans appear to respect this decision. Surely, this is what makes the little snippets of information that the singer is happy to share all the more precious.

Opening Up

'Whenever I'm out in public, I have to be put together. When I get home, I rebel against it and I don't want to take care of anything. I drop it. I'm relaxed. I don't have any shoes on. No makeup.'

Who can imagine *that* Beyoncé? And perhaps that is the point. When the door closes, when those heels come off, we don't know who Beyoncé Knowles is. And, almost definitely, that is part of the appeal: a mystique that in an age of reality TV and magazine deals we rarely get from our pop stars.

For years Beyoncé did not even acknowledge her relationship with the future father of her children; her private life was exactly that: private. However, since she and Jay-Z got married in 2008 – and even more so since the pair had their daughter Blue Ivy – that side of her life has been

'We took our time and developed an unbreakable friendship before we got married. I admire his ability to inspire others.'

BEYONCÉ

'The most amazing feeling I feel/Words can't describe the feeling, for real/ Baby, I paint the sky blue/My greatest creation was you.'

JAY-Z'S 'GLORY', ABOUT THE BIRTH OF HIS DAUGHTER

acknowledged a lot more. In fact, in 2013 she made her biggest public acknowledgement of her husband to date by announcing the name of her new tour: the Mrs Carter Show.

The new moniker split fans; some of them felt that taking Jay-Z's name in this way was an anti-feminist statement, whereas others loved it as a cheeky acknowledgment of a new phase in Beyoncé's life.

The Anti-Rihanna?

Meanwhile, Bey was taking small steps to reveal bits of her life to her fans by making clever choices with a website full of quality images of her family, rather than the ubiquitous Twitter feed favoured by many of her contemporaries (did somebody say Rihanna?).

Instead of getting bored by relentless images, fans end up craving more, loving the authenticity of the pictures and posts, and the beautiful images of family life. Beyoncé has been praised for how she has been using social media and heralded as someone who really knows how to build a brand. In fact, social media Beyoncé has a lot in common with real life Beyoncé: classy, beautiful and only willing to reveal as much as she is comfortable with when it comes to that all-important home life.

The same is true of Beyoncé's attitude to her daughter. Blue's birth in January 2012 was shrouded in mystery, with heavy security and rumours that the couple had rented out an entire floor of the Lenox Hill Hospital, before the first pictures of her

'We welcome you to share in our joy. Thank you for respecting our privacy at this beautiful time in our lives. The Carter family.'

appeared on Bey and Jay-Z's own terms. It was notable that the couple did not sign a magazine deal for these pictures – not the Carters' style – but posted them for free on their website.

No Suri Cruise

In the documentary 'Life Is But A Dream', Beyoncé acknowledged the internet rumours that she had faked her pregnancy with Blue and actually used a surrogate, saying they were 'the most ridiculous rumours I've ever heard of me … to think I'd be that vain'.

A few days after Blue's birth, Jay-Z paid tribute in his own way and wrote the song 'Glory', which celebrated his daughter's birth through its lyrics. And now? Well, Blue Ivy may be a known (very cute) face, but she is a world away from being a Suri Cruise, i.e. a celebrity child whose face becomes so recognizable that they become famous in their own right.

Instead, we see Blue when Beyoncé and Jay-Z say it's OK, and when they decide to give us a glimpse of their daughter – and in between those appearances, the family live their life as they always have: firmly behind closed doors.

'I feel like Mrs Carter is who I am, but more bold and more fearless than I've ever been.' BEYONCÉ

'As a young girl I remember seeing so many artists, and then I'd try to dress like them.'

BEYONCÉ

How Does She Look?

Effortlessly beautiful – with or without makeup – Beyoncé would look good wearing anything but her great taste means that certain items of clothing that she chose for her videos have become almost as famous as her songs. Nowadays, though, Bey no longer just wears the clothes: she also designs them, demonstrating once again how versatile her talents are.

Crazy In Style

Beyoncé admits that her music and her style go hand in hand; when she hears a single, she immediately knows the look that will go with it. It makes sense, really – who can imagine the 'Single Ladies' video without the one-shouldered bodysuit or 'Crazy In Love' without the denim hot pants and vest ('I wanted to be a female version of James Dean') strutting towards us?

'I always think about wearing something a fan could buy and make her own,' Beyoncé told *W* magazine in 2011. The videos are one thing but when it comes to the tour outfits, there is not much chance of teenagers recreating the looks at home – not unless they have some pretty impressive talents. Case in point: the gold sequinned bodysuit with the trompe l'oeil breasts from the Mrs Carter Show that took away attention from the gorgeous white Ralph and Russo look because … well didn't you hear what it involved? The looks have become part of the show, as big an event as the performance itself.

Getting It Wrong

But where Beyoncé's style has led, a divisive reaction has always followed. Like a lot of people who have been famous from a young age, she has not always got it right – hard as that is to believe when she is shimmering down a red carpet in a Givenchy.

Although now designers are clearly clamouring to lend to Beyoncé, in the early days of Destiny's Child they wouldn't even lend to the band. She has some favourites (Givenchy is a regular) and Beyoncé pays personal visits to Azzedine Alaia himself to pick up some pieces. 'She doesn't have the body of a typical model, but she inspires the designers,' creative director Jenke-Ahmed Tailly who worked with Beyoncé told *Harper's Bazaar*.

On The Other Side

These days, of course, Bey goes beyond wearing the clothes; she is on the other side. As well as working with H&M – she signed a deal as the face of the brand in 2013 – Beyoncé has her own clothing range, House of Deréon, which she runs with her stylist and designer mum, Tina. It is a proper family business – where Bey's sister Solange often models – and was inspired by their grandmother, the late Agnèz Deréon.

It was in 2013, though, that Bey really 'arrived' in fashion circles. Being invited to be the Honorary Chair of the

Metropolitan Museum of Art Costume Institute Gala, hosted annually by American *Vogue* editor Anna Wintour, was a sign that Beyoncé was now being taken seriously by the fashion set.

Of course, one of the most amazing things about Beyoncé is that also when away from the red carpet, she can frequently look as gorgeous as she does on it – even when she's wearing jeans and no makeup. That's the power of that body and, of course, that incredible face.

She was named *People* magazine's Most Beautiful Woman 2012 but lost out to her good friend Gwyneth Paltrow the year later; imagine the rise in temperature in the room when *they* get together – even if they are in sweatpants! That was also the year when she had her daughter and Beyoncé does not believe that's a coincidence, crediting Blue with bringing out a true beauty that did not exist before she became a mother.

'My fans kept asking where they could get clothes like Destiny's Child's, so it was only natural for us to do a clothing line.'

BEYONCÉ

'[My mother is] gifted, and it just was natural for us to do this line because this is our life.'

BEYONCÉ ON HOUSE OF DERÉON

YONCÉ

'I feel more beautiful than I've
ever felt because I've given birth.
I have never felt so connected ...
like I had such a purpose.'

BEYONCÉ

Say It Loud

All those who simply dismiss Beyoncé as just another pretty face couldn't be more wrong: she strongly champions some very important causes and charities close to her heart. And it's not just her millions of fans who take her seriously: her friendship with the US President and the First Lady underlines exactly how far she has risen.

Putting A Ring On It

'If you like it, you should be able to put a ring on it,' said Beyoncé's handwritten note, posted on Instagram with the hashtag #wewillunite4marriageequality. She had previously been vocal about her belief that preventing gay people from getting married is equivalent to racism: another form of prejudice. 'It's no different than discriminating against blacks,' she told CNN. 'It's discrimination, plain and simple.'

It's not all just about hot pants and fierce dances; increasingly, Beyoncé uses her fame for a greater good, championing important causes that matter to her.

Demanding A Plan

We had seen it with gun control too; along with other big names, such as Reese Witherspoon and Selena Gomez,

'When you look around at all that's wrong in the world, the need to do something, no matter how big or how small, is clear.'

BEYONCÉ

'Barack's just a very special person and he was born to do what he does, and Michelle was born to do what she does.'

BEYONCÉ

Bey lent her name to 'Demand A Plan', which called for changes in gun laws after the horrific shooting at Sandy Hook school in December 2012.

Beyoncé has always been a philanthropist and nowhere was that more evident than when she and her family, including fellow Destiny's girl Kelly Rowland, founded the Survivor Foundation: a charity that endeavours to help victims to get back on their feet after disasters. Originally launched after Hurricane Katrina, the charity has raised millions.

Reaching Out

It's much more low key than her world tours, or her album releases, but Beyoncé's humanitarian work is just as epic and wide-reaching. As part of the post-hurricane effort, Beyoncé, along with Kelly, also donated a large amount of money to an affordable housing initiative –the Knowles-Rowland Temenos Place Apartments in Houston – which provides accommodation to people after natural or personal disasters.

In 2010 Beyoncé and her mum opened the Beyoncé Cosmetology Centre at the Brooklyn Phoenix House, which treats men and women with drug and alcohol addiction. The idea was to provide vocational beauty training to people at Phoenix House, where Beyoncé initially visited as part of her research for a film role. Close to tears at the opening, Beyoncé said: 'I felt like they needed something that was geared towards women – something that would teach them skills that would give them hope even after the Phoenix House.'

'To J and B, thank you so much for your friendship. Beyoncé could not be a better role model for my girls.'

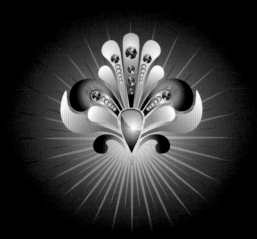

'My parents taught my sister and me the importance of giving back and making a difference in another person's life.'

Beyoncé also took part in Wyclef Jean and George Clooney's Haiti benefit, and was an ambassador for World Humanitarian Day. She may not shout about it as loudly as Angelina does, but Beyoncé is arguably one of the most charitable celebrities out there.

Two First Ladies

In 2013 Beyoncé threw her weight behind her latest initiative: Chime for Change – a global campaign for girls' and women's empowerment that's been termed 'Feminist Live Aid'. The pinnacle was a concert on 1 June which saw Beyoncé and other female heavyweights perform in London.

All of this obviously plays a key part in the close relationship that Beyoncé has with the US President and his wife, which began, really, with a simple case of mutual appreciation: Beyoncé is a great supporter of Obama and the President believes that Beyoncé is a great idol for his two young daughters.

When Beyoncé sung Etta James's 'At Last' at Obama's inauguration, it was a seminal moment. It also led to the singer performing at the President's second inauguration, where she sang the National Anthem.

When Jay-Z hosted a fundraiser for the Obamas in 2012, the President took to the microphone and thanked both singers for their friendship. It went further than that: the couple are so tight with the President and the First Lady that Obama used nicknames in his speech, referring to them as 'J and B'. If they did not know they'd made it before … yes, that would do it.

> 'Yes, I am powerful.
> I'm more powerful than
> my mind can even digest
> and understand.'
>
> BEYONCÉ

In Full Flight

Through the ups and downs of 2013, Beyoncé has emerged as a strong, confident and ever more popular superstar. What is going to happen next? We can only wait and see …

World Takeover

If something is having a moment now, Beyoncé is usually involved. She bagged the 2013 Grammy for Best Traditional R&B Performance (for 'Love On Top') and pride of place on the soundtrack of 2013's biggest film release: *The Great Gatsby* with her cover of Amy Winehouse's 'Back to Black'. Turn the TV on and there is a Beyoncé Pepsi advert; go shopping and she's staring at you in a bikini in H&M. When the biggest concert of the year was planned? You know who was leading from the front.

MisBeyhaving

However, 2013 wasn't all easy. Criticized for visiting Cuba, due to the US ban on travel to the country, Beyoncé also hit the headlines when she banned press photographers from her tour after a few … let's call them 'funny' facial expressions were caught on camera and featured on websites around the world. For the first time ever, she also cancelled a gig on doctors' orders – which fuelled the pregnancy rumours – in Antwerp.

'I feel really, really just lucky that I can still do what I love, and now have a way bigger meaning. And that's to be her [Blue's] mother.'

BEYONCÉ

Perhaps the biggest controversy, though, came when she performed 'The Star-Spangled Banner' at the second inauguration of President Obama. It was an innocent comment by a spokesperson for the US Marine band – saying that Beyoncé 'decided to go with the pre-recorded music at the last minute' – that kicked the whole thing off. The next minute it had made the news around the world.

However, this Beyoncé is a different entity from the one who struggled to cope during the Destiny's Child years. You get the impression that Sasha Fierce is no longer just an alter ego but has become part of Beyoncé. She kept quiet for two weeks and then in front of reporters at a press conference she belted out a note-perfect version of 'The Star-Spangled Banner', finishing with the words: 'Any questions?'

'I am a perfectionist,' she explained, 'and one thing about me, I practice until my feet bleed, and I did not have time to rehearse with the orchestra … due to no proper sound check, I did not feel comfortable taking a risk … So I decided to sing along with my pre-recorded track, which is very common in the music industry.'

'When I leave this world, I'll leave no regrets/Leave something to remember, so they won't forget /I was here.' BEYONCÉ, 'I WAS HERE'

She then, of course, sang live at the Super Bowl, doing an energetic medley of tracks including 'Crazy In Love' and 'Baby Boy', and not missing a note, before the *pièce de résistance*: the arrival of Michelle and Kelly for a Destiny's Child medley. Without a doubt one of the most iconic performances of all time, the girls went into 'Independent Women', 'Bootylicious' and ended with a version of 'Single Ladies', complete, of course, with *The Dance*. At the end, Beyoncé announced her world tour.

A Megastar For A New Generation

Consensus from those who saw the Mrs Carter tour was that there could be no better: Bey was a superstar – a megastar for a new generation. 'She had a star wattage that was blinding, an ability to sing and dance and be mesmerizing,' said one review.

But what about the now surely overdue fifth album? Don't worry, everyone, Gwyneth tells us that it is definitely coming soon – and if anyone knows, it's Gwyneth. And after that? Well, we could expect anything, as Beyoncé's own words tell us: 'I'm telling my daughter every day, "You know you can be president, you know it's possible,"' she says. Beyoncé for president? You wouldn't bet against it.

'I would like more children. I think my daughter needs some company. I love being a big sister.' BEYONCÉ

Beyoncé Vital Info

Birth Name   Beyoncé Giselle Knowles

Birth Date   4 September 1981

Birth Place   Houston, Texas, USA

Nationality   American

Height   1.67 m (5 ft 6 in)

Hair Colour   Golden Brown

Eye Colour   Hazel

Discography

Albums

Dangerously In Love (2003)

B'Day (2006)

I Am ... Sasha Fierce (2008)

4 (2011)

Singles

2002:   'Work It Out' (UK No. 7)

'03 Bonnie & Clyde' (Jay-Z featuring Beyoncé) (UK No. 2, US No. 4)

2003:   'Crazy In Love' (featuring Jay-Z) (UK No. 1, US No. 1)

'Baby Boy' (featuring Sean Paul) (UK No. 2, US No. 1)

'Me, Myself and I' (UK No. 4)

2004:   'Naughty Girl' (UK No. 10, US No. 3)

2005:   'Check On It' (featuring Slim Thug) (UK No. 3, US No. 1)

2006:   'Déjà Vu' (featuring Jay-Z) (UK No. 1, US No. 4)

'Irreplaceable' (UK No. 4, US No. 1)

2007:   'Listen' (UK No. 8)

'Beautiful Liar' (with Shakira) (UK No. 1, US No. 3)

2008:   'If I Were A Boy' (UK No. 1, US No. 3)

'Single Ladies (Put A Ring On It)' (UK No. 7, US No. 1)

2009:   'Halo' (UK No. 4, US No. 5)

'Sweet Dreams' (UK No. 5, US No. 10)

2010:   'Telephone' (Lady Gaga featuring Beyoncé) (UK No. 1, US No. 3)

2011:   'Run The World (Girls)' (UK No. 11)

'Best Thing I Never Had' (UK No. 3)

Awards

American Music Awards

2007:   International Artist Award

2009:   Favorite Soul/R&B Female Artist

2011:   Favorite Soul/R&B Female Artist

2012:   Favorite Soul/R&B Female Artist

BET Awards

2004:   Best Collaboration 'Crazy in Love' (featuring Jay-Z)

2006:   Best Female R&B Artist

2007:   Video of the Year 'Irreplaceable'

Best Female R&B Artist

2009:   Best Female R&B Artist

Video of the Year 'Single Ladies' (Put A Ring On It)

2010:   Video of the Year 'Video Phone (featuring Lady Gaga)

2011:   Best Female R&B Artist

2012: Video Director of the Year Beyoncé and Alan Ferguson 'Love On Top'

Billboard Music Awards
2003: New Female Artist

Hot 100 Female Artist

Hot 100 Award for Most Weeks at No.1 ('Crazy In Love' and 'Baby Boy')

New R&B Artist

2009: Billboard Woman of the Year Award

2011: Billboard Millennium Award

2012: Top R&B Album *4*

Brit Awards
2004: Best International Female Solo Artist

Grammy Awards
2004: Best R&B Song 'Crazy In Love' (featuring Jay-Z)

Best Rap/Sung Collaboration 'Crazy In Love' (featuring Jay-Z)

Best Female R&B Vocal Performance 'Dangerously In Love 2'

Best R&B Performance by a Duo or Group with Vocals 'The Closer I Get To You' (with Luther Vandross)

Best Contemporary R&B Album *Dangerously In Love*

2007: Best Contemporary R&B Album *B'Day*

2009: Best Contemporary R&B Album *I Am … Sasha Fierce*

Best Female Pop Vocal Performance 'Halo'

2010: Song of the Year 'Single Ladies (Put A Ring On It)'

Best R&B Song 'Single Ladies (Put A Ring On It)'

Best Female R&B Vocal Performance 'Single Ladies (Put A Ring On It)'

Best Traditional R&B Vocal Performance 'At Last'

2013: Best Traditional R&B Vocal Performance 'Love On Top'

Ivor Novello Awards
2008: Best-Selling British Single 'Beautiful Liar' (with Shakira)

MOBO Awards
2006: Best Song 'Déjà Vu' (featuring Jay-Z)

Best Video 'Déjà Vu' (featuring Jay-Z)

Best International Female Artist

2009: Best Video 'Single Ladies (Put A Ring On It)'

Best International Act

MTV Music Video Awards
2003: Best Female Video 'Crazy In Love' (featuring Jay-Z)

Best R&B Video 'Crazy In Love' (featuring Jay-Z)

Best Choreography 'Crazy In Love' (featuring Jay-Z)

2004: Best Female Video 'Naughty Girl'

2006: Best R&B Video 'Check On It' (featuring Slim Thug)

2007: Most Earthshattering Collaboration 'Beautiful Liar' (with Shakira)

2009: Video of the Year 'Single Ladies (Put A Ring On It)'

Best Editing 'Single Ladies (Put A Ring On It)'

Best Choreography 'Single Ladies (Put A Ring On It)'

2010: Best Collaboration 'Telephone' (with Lady Gaga)

2011: Best Choreography 'Run The World (Girls)'

2012: Best Editing 'Countdown'

MTV Europe Music Awards
2003: Best Song 'Crazy In Love' (featuring Jay-Z)

Best R&B

2009: Best Female

Best Video 'Single Ladies (Put A Ring On It)'

Best Song 'Halo'

Teen Choice Awards
2003: Choice Love Song 'Crazy In Love' (featuring Jay-Z)

Choice Summer Song 'Crazy In Love' (featuring Jay-Z)

2009: Choice Music: R&B Artist

Choice Music: R&B Track 'Single Ladies (Put A Ring On It)'

2010: Choice Music: R&B Artist

2011: Choice Music: R&B/Hip-Hop Track 'Run The World (Girls)'

Tours

Dangerously In Love Tour: November 2003; Europe
Verizon Ladies First Tour: March–April 2004; North America
The Beyoncé Experience: April–December 2007; Worldwide
I Am … Tour: March 2009–February 2010; Worldwide
The Mrs Carter Show World Tour: April–September 2013 (Worldwide)

Online

www.beyonce.com:
Beyoncé's official site packed with all the must know information about the global superstar including tour dates.

@Beyonce:
Join millions of others and follow Beyoncé's very own Twitter updates.

www.facebook.com/beyonce:
With millions of likes and thousands of photos, Beyoncé's Facebook page has everything an adoring fan will need to know about the girl herself with exclusive posts and updates.

www.youtube.com/artist/beyoncé:
Beyoncé's official YouTube channel is packed with all the singer's music videos.

Caroline Corcoran

Caroline Corcoran is a freelance writer and editor who has previously worked at *3am Online*, *More!*, *Sugar*, *Fabulous* and *Heat*. She now writes for a variety of publications and websites on celebrity, TV, popular culture, any issues that are relevant to women, and most things that people are gossiping about on Twitter. She is also writing her first novel. Follow her on Twitter @cgcorcoran

Malcolm Mackenzie (Foreword)

Malcolm Mackenzie is the editor of *We Love Pop*. He started as a professional pop fan writing for teen titles like *Top of the Pops*, *Bliss* and *TV Hits* before moving into the adult market working for *GQ*, *Glamour*, *Grazia*, *Attitude*, and newspapers such as *The Times*, *The Sunday Times*, *The Guardian* and *thelondonpaper* where he was Music Editor for three years before returning to the teen sector to launch *We Love Pop*.

Picture Credits

All images © Getty Images: Tony Barson Archive/WireImage: 90; Bryan Bedder: 18, 120; Al Bello: 118; Vince Bucci: 35, 84, 110, 128; Larry Busacca/WireImage: 3, 16, 26, 70, 93, 123; Matt Cardy: 86; Michael Caulfield Archive/WireImage: 40; Gregg DeGuire/WireImage: 108; Kristian Dowling: 88; Tabatha Fireman/Redferns: 102; Ian Gavan: 56, 113 (for Gucci); Steve Granitz/WireImage: 6, 13, 29, 126; Scott Gries: 14; Dave Hogan: 7; Samir Hussein: 106; Dimitrios Kambouris: 61, 105; Jason Kempin/FilmMagic: 78, 98; Jeff Kravitz/FilmMagic: 50; Mike Lawrie: 10; Paul McConnell: 30; Eamonn McCormack/WireImage: 117; Kevin Mazur/WireImage: 4, 8, 22, 25, 36, 38, 44, 49, 52, 58, 64, 67, 68, 72, 94, 101, 114, 124; Jason Merritt: Cover, 21; Frank Micelotta: 46; Getty Images: 77; Al Pereira/WireImage: 43; Christopher Polk: 1, 74; Jun Sato/WireImage: 54; John Shearer/WireImage: 96; Jason Squires/WireImage: 87; Venturelli/WireImage: 83; Mark Wilson: 80; Kevin Winter: 32, 62